KNOW WHAT I MEAN?

Poems selected by Pie Corbett

CONTENTS

Stevie Scared

Stevie Scared, scared of the dark,
Scared of rats, of dogs that bark,
Scared of his fat dad, scared of his mother,
Scared of his sis and his tattooed brother,
Scared of tall girls, scared of boys,
Scared of ghosts and sudden noise,
Scared of spiders, scared of bees,
Scared of standing under trees,
Scared of shadows, scared of adders,
Scared of the devil, scared of ladders,
Scared of hailstones, scared of rain,
Scared of falling down the drain,
Stevie Scared, scared of showing
He's so scared and people knowing,
Spends his whole time kicking, fighting,
Shoving, pinching, butting, biting,
Bashing little kids about
(Just in case they find him out).

Richard Edwards

PLAYGROUNDS

Playgrounds are such gobby places.
Know what I mean?
Everyone seems to have something to
Talk about, giggle, whisper, scream and shout about.
I mean, it's like being in a parrot cage.

And playgrounds are such pushy places.
Know what I mean?
Everyone seems to have to
Run about, jump, kick, do cartwheels, handstands, fly around.
I mean, it's like being inside a whirlwind.

And playgrounds are such patchy places.
Know what I mean?
Everyone seems to
Go round in circles, lines and triangles, coloured shapes.
I mean, it's like being in a kaleidoscope.

And playgrounds are such pally places.
Know what I mean?
Everyone seems to
Have best friends, secrets, link arms, be in gangs.
Everyone except me.
Know what I mean?

Berlie Doherty

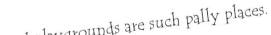

3

BIG Hole

My best friend Jenny Colquhoun has moved on.
She's gone to live in a posher part of town.
She left a big hole; an empty space next to my desk.
My hands hold themselves on the way to school.

But see in her new house she has a dining room,
a TV room – imagine a room just for watching! –
and her own bedroom. I stayed the night;
got lost on my way back from the bathroom.

I was there the day before her ninth birthday.
I was the special friend from the old school.
But when her new friends came they stared
till I thought I should check the mirror, as if

I had a big hole in my tights. 'What did you
get Jenny for her birthday?' *'Anne of Green Gables'*,
I said, burning under the wrong dress,
wanting the thick carpet to swallow me up.

'Have you always been that colour?' says the one
with the freckles. And a giggle spreads from room
to room till Jenny's beautiful red-haired mother
saves me: *'Anne of Green Gables*? A wonderful book.'

Jackie Kay

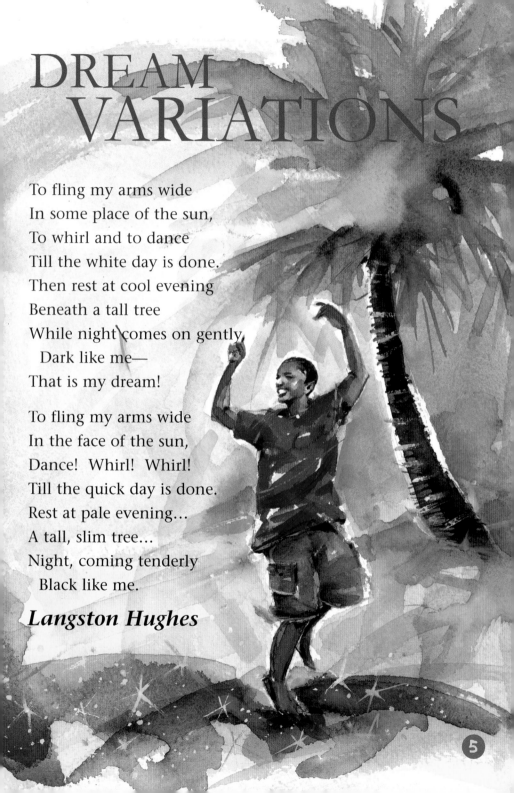

DREAM VARIATIONS

To fling my arms wide
In some place of the sun,
To whirl and to dance
Till the white day is done.
Then rest at cool evening
Beneath a tall tree
While night comes on gently,
  Dark like me—
That is my dream!

To fling my arms wide
In the face of the sun,
Dance! Whirl! Whirl!
Till the quick day is done.
Rest at pale evening...
A tall, slim tree...
Night, coming tenderly
  Black like me.

Langston Hughes

The Purse

I pinched it from my mother's purse,
Pretending it's a game.
My muscles tightened: hard and tense.
I pinched it just the same.

'I need it as a loan,' I said.
'It's not against the law.'
'I won't do it again,' I said.
I've said all that before.

The reason was the cash at first,
It isn't any more;
I do it…well…because I do,
I don't know what it's for.

I only know that when the house
Is silent, empty, still,
I head towards my parents' room
As if against my will.

The sweat is cold upon my neck,
My back and arms feel strange,
I'm sure that someone's watching me
As I pick out her change.

But no one ever catches me,
Sometimes I wish they would;
Then perhaps I'd stop and think
And give it up for good.

But my mum trusts me, buys me things:
Each kindness makes it worse
Because I know, when she's next door
My hands will find her purse.

David Kitchen

STAR GAZING

At midnight through my window
I spy with wondering eye
The far-off stars and planets
Sprinkled on the sky.

There the constant North Star
Hangs above our trees
And there the Plough and Sirius
And the distant Pleiades.

Star on star counting
Each one a raging sun
And the sky one endless suburb
With all her lights left on.

How strange it is that certain stars
Whose distant lights still glow
Vanished in that sea of space
Three million years ago.

And if I stare too long a time
The stars swim in my eyes
Drifting towards my bedroom
down the vast slope of the skies.

And, mesmerized, I wonder,
Will *our* Earth someday die?
Spreading her fabric and her dreams
In fragments on the sky.

And then my imagination
Sees in some distant dawn
A young girl staring skywards
On a planet still unborn.

And will she also wonder,
Was there ever life out there?
Before the whole thing vanished
Like a dream into the air.

Gareth Owen

The River

The River's a wanderer,
A nomad, a tramp,
He doesn't choose one place
To set up his camp.

The River's a winder,
Through valley and hill
He twists and he turns,
He just cannot be still.

The River's a hoarder,
And he buries down deep
Those little treasures
That he wants to keep.

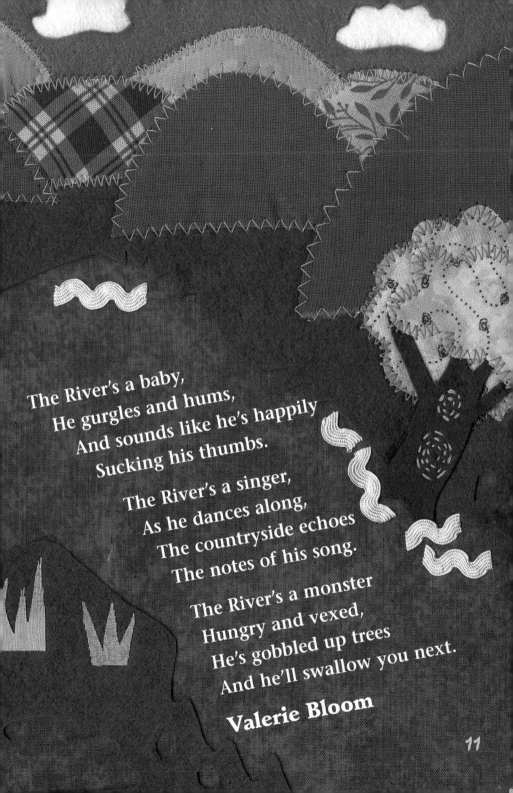

The River's a baby,
He gurgles and hums,
And sounds like he's happily
Sucking his thumbs.

The River's a singer,
As he dances along,
The countryside echoes
The notes of his song.

The River's a monster
Hungry and vexed,
He's gobbled up trees
And he'll swallow you next.

Valerie Bloom

April Rain Song

Let the rain kiss you.

Let the rain beat upon your head with silver liquid drops.

Let the rain sing you a lullaby.

The rain makes still pools on the sidewalk,

The rain makes running pools in the gutter.

The rain plays a little sleep-song on our roof at night –

And I love the rain.

Langston Hughes

SONG OF THE SKY LOOM

O our Mother the Earth, O our Father the Sky,
Your children are we, and with tired backs
We bring you the gifts you love.
Then weave for us a garment of brightness;
May the warp be the white light of morning,
May the weft be the red light of evening,
May the fringes be the falling rain,
May the border be the standing rainbow.
Thus weave for us a garment of brightness,
That we may walk fittingly where grass is green,
O our Mother the Earth, O our Father the Sky.

Tewa (North American Indian)

NIGHT CAT

She's there by the fence
but you mustn't call out,
like a scoop of night
or a water shadow
tense for flight
she'll twist and go,
don't open your mouth –
the moon's so close
that the stars blow out –
leaving that patch
where the moon shone
leaving the empty
dress of night
with the stars picked out
and you alone.

Helen Dunmore

On a Night of Snow

Cat, if you go outdoors, you must walk in the snow.
You will come back with little white shoes on your feet,
little white shoes of snow that have heels of sleet.
Stay by the fire, my Cat. Lie still, do not go.
See how the flames are leaping and hissing low,
I will bring you a saucer of milk like a marguerite,
so white and so smooth, so spherical and so sweet –
stay with me, Cat. Outdoors the wild winds blow.

Outdoors the wild winds blow, Mistress, and dark is the night,
strange voices cry in the trees, intoning strange lore,
and more than cats move, lit by our eyes' green light,
on silent feet where the meadow grasses hang hoar –
Mistress, there are portents abroad of magic and might,
and things that are yet to be done. Open the door!

Elizabeth Coatsworth

ALONE LOOKING AT THE MOUNTAIN

All the birds have flown up and gone;
A lonely cloud floats leisurely by.
We never tire of looking at each other —
Only the mountain and I.

Li Bai

Under the cloudy cliff, near the temple door,
Between dusky spring plants on the pond,
A frog jumps in the water, plop!
Startled, the poet drops his brush.

Sengai

TEACHER

Loud shouter
Deep thinker
Rain hater
Coffee drinker

Spell checker
Sum ticker
Line giver
Nit picker

Ready listener
Trouble carer
Hometime lover
Knowledge sharer

Paul Cookson

ICICLE

Sue Cowling

long
tooth,
witch's
nail,
tip
of an
ice-
dragon's
tail,
sharp
horn,
drip
that
froze
at the
end of
an ice-
troll's
nose
!

Magic

A web
captures the storm:
glass beads, safe in fine net,
gather sunlight as they sway in
high winds.

Judith Nicholls

ON SIDE CINQUAIN

The ball
went splat against
the garage wall then bounced
down to my right toe. Goalie had
no chance!

Matt Simpson

SPANISH HOLIDAY HAIKU

Flies stalk the cup's rim –
washing their hands, fidgeting
in the sullen heat.

The sun sweats, hills shake.
The landscape does nothing too.
The pool is ice cool.

Distant hill lies still
like a sleeping lion, crouching.
An eagle hovers.

Pencil dragonflies,
in slim, pastel blue hover,
shivering, pool-side.

Daisy's wasp sting –
like a white injection mark –
a white raised moon.

Trying to sleep but
the room is far too stuffy –
even pillows sweat.

PIE CORBETT

PLEASE NOAH!
TORTOISE

I'm slow, Noah,
slow.
Don't put me near
the hare,
the horse's hoof,
the elephant.
Please let me share my room
with someone small:
with mole, light-footed wren
or snail – he cannot stamp
or run. Best of all,
just let me be
alone.

Judith Nicholls

THE BLACKBIRD'S EPITAPH

Beneath this mound of earth
there lies
A song that filled
the morning skies.
May none of us
forsake our tree
Till we have given
as much as he.

Sue Cowling

Index of Titles